Critical Thinking

Powerful Strategies That Will Make You Improve Decisions And Think Smarter

Harvey Segler

Table of contents

FREE Bonus!

<u>Want to make money while you sleep?</u>

Visit >>><u>www.GreenSleeper.com</u><<< to get free tips about how you can make serious money while doing anything else! Sleeping, laying on the beach, traveling, only your imagination is the limit!

At the moment you can get a FREE download of:

"The Make Money While You Sleep Guide"

But hurry up, the book will not be there forever!

Visit My Website And Download It Now! 100% Free! What Do You Have To Lose? Just Search www.GreenSleeper.com In Your Web Browser!

If you don't want the book, read the blog which can teach you a lot of things about business, time management, performance and other things connected to business and success.

Introduction

I want to thank you and congratulate you for downloading the book, Critical Thinking.

This book contains proven steps and strategies on how to help you improve how you make decisions and think about things smarter. We all want to make good decisions in our life, and make those decisions in full confidence that we are doing the right thing.

Imagine a life where you didn't have to guess with your decisions. You were able to think about situations in ways that gave you control of or influence over the outcome.

That is what this book is about. In it you will learn how to think about life in a whole new way. You will learn how to view decisions and situations in ways that you never thought you would before.

From forming your own opinions and independent thinking to making decisions that will have greater benefits for you, the lessons you will find in this book are proven strategies that will help you improve your critical thinking.

Within days you are going to see that your decision making skills are going to greatly increase, and you are going to feel a lot more confident with your choices.

Thanks again for getting this book, I hope you enjoy it!

Chapter 1 – What Is Critical Thinking?

Critical thinking is a concept that is intimidating to a lot of people. As soon as they hear the word "critical", their mind goes to somewhere intense and above their level. When you combine that with "thinking", you cause a lot of people to shy away from the concept altogether.

There are a lot of ideas and premonitions that surround the concept of critical thinking, but while the prejudices range from a bunch of science geeks surrounding a table in white lab coats to politicians debating the laws of the country, the phrase itself has a simple meaning.

"Critical thinking" is defined as: *The objective analysis and evaluation of an issue in order to form a judgement.*

Confused? Don't be. This is merely a lot of large words to describe what is really a very simple concept. Simple in practice, that is, because you could be thinking about anything, whether that be a faster way to get to work in the morning, or something as difficult as curing cancer.

As intimidating as this concept sounds, it is really quite simple when it comes to the practice of it.

Critical thinking is a combination of two separate acts:

1. Absorbing Information
2. Putting that information to good use

This is so much more than just reading facts, or watching a documentary, or even wishing that you could do this better or that better. There is a difference between *seeing* something and *absorbing* it.

Naturally, we are inclined to see something, then forget about it. Sure, we might hang on to a bit of interesting information here and there, but it is unusual for anyone to take in the world and process it in their minds in a useful sort of way.

We would all rather 'wow' our friends with something we heard or read as opposed to actually learning something useful and putting that knowledge to good work in our day to day lives.

Then again, there are many out there that *do* want to learn. They want to be able to read and retain, then apply that to their life in a way that is actually useful to them in a variety of ways.

Critical thinking goes hand in hand with independent thinking. If you are a critical thinker, you are able to think for yourself, and form your own opinions. You are able to take in a subject or a situation, evaluate the facts, and draw your own conclusions.

These conclusions may or may not match with what other people have decided, but that isn't anything that you concern yourself with. You know what you saw, and you know how you feel about it. As a result, you are independent and believe what you believe regardless of what others are saying.

This isn't saying that the other people are wrong, it is merely saying that you are able to make your own opinions, and stand by them. There is nothing at all wrong with agreeing with other people, and there isn't anything wrong with disagreeing.

You may be surprised to find out how many critical thinkers there are in the world, they are just good at what they do.

There are a lot of independent thinkers out there, but not many people realize that they are. If you stop and think about it for a second. There is someone behind every ad campaign, and someone behind all of the elections. When you are talking to a salesman that is trying to sell you his own product, or when you see the rise of a new social empire.

These may not feel like they are independent, especially when you see all of the people that are getting on board, but what you have to remember is that there is a free thinker behind it all, and that person is telling everyone else what to think. The problem for the rest of the world is that these people are good at telling others what to think, and it isn't long before you have an entire group that is only doing what they are told, because they are told to think it.

What our goal is here is to teach you how to take in a situation and form *your own opinion* from that situation, regardless of what that opinion may be.

Now, you may find this scary, or you could find it exciting. We want you to be able to think for yourself on any topic. In fact, we want the entire world to be able to think for itself.

There are tons of people out there that don't care what happens on this planet. They go through their lives day in and day out being spoon fed whatever it is society wants to tell them, with little thought of ever doing anything better, or anything at all, for that matter.

Then there are those that aren't happy just going with the flow. They know that there is something better in life, and that they have the ability to get it, they just don't know how.

It is to these people that this book is directed. We are going to explore what it takes to absorb information, and show you ways that you can then apply what you learn to your life. It doesn't matter what you are learning, or what you wish to do with this information.

It is a method that you need to learn, and in the chapters to come we are going to go through the steps that it is going to take for you to learn that information.

Chapter 2 – The Three Steps To Independent Thinking

As soon as you wake up in the morning, you are hit with opinions. All kinds of news and thoughts and opinions come pouring into your mind whether it be from family, television, the radio, or work.

You are hit with advertisements and other social media... all of which are competing for your attention. For those that are just going through the motions, this is a lot of noise. They are told to think this or to prefer that.

They end up going for what is the shiniest, just because it is the shiniest. They don't know a thing about any of their choices, they are just doing what they are told. That is where critical and independent thinking come in.

You need to train your mind to think for itself, it isn't something that is just going to happen. Unfortunately, by default we are going to go with what is easiest in life, and that tends to be whatever everyone else is doing, regardless of what it is they are doing.

You need to learn how to break that cycle. In order to do that, you need to learn to sift through the information you are receiving, and pick out what is important.

There are going to be so many opinions and different suggestions that are thrown in your face in a day, you won't have time to process it all. This means that you need to learn the art of sifting through the information that is given you, and pick out the important stuff.

Pay attention to the details that matter in your day, and forget about the rest. If it doesn't affect you or what you are doing, that is your first clue that it needs to be placed low on your priority list.

But how can you know what information you should pay attention to, and what you should discard?

It is a tricky thing to get the hang of, but with practice, you are going to get it. Here is a list of the top 3 ways you can get through all of the information that is tossed your way in a day, and find what is actually relevant to you and your life.

Keep in mind, however, that if a person is making a point of saying something, they are probably benefiting from it in some way. Some information can become very convincing simply because of the passion of the person that is presenting the information.

These steps are going to help you pick through all kinds of information you are met with in a day, and find what is relevant to your situation, regardless of how convincing the voice is of the speaker.

Step 1. Consider the motive of the speaker.

As we have already pointed out, when an individual is making a point to say something, odds are they are going to be benefiting from it in some way. They may be trying to sell you an item, or they may want something from you.

With this in mind, take everything you read and hear with a grain of salt. There is probably some truth to what the person is saying, but that truth has likely been tampered with. There may be aspects about it that are left out, there may be things that are embellished.

It is unusual for people in this situation to make an outright lie, but it certainly isn't unheard of. You don't want to be distrustful of everyone that you meet, but you do want to be aware the world isn't all just there to give you information and opinions, odds are there is a secondary motive of some kind that is asking for something from you in return.

Step 2. Consider the source of the information.

A lot of people just pull ideas out of their minds and spout them off as truth. This is something that people have done for hundreds of years... it is human nature. Information such as this has become more readily available to the world thanks to inventions such as the internet.

You have to remember that just because someone says something, that doesn't make it true. The same rule goes for whether or not you see something that is online. Just because you read it, that doesn't make it true.

If you hear or read something, and it just seems 'off' in some way, go with your gut feeling on that. Unless you see that there are credible sources or proof behind the information, then question it.

Never just blindly believe anything. If something is legitimate, then there is going to be genuine and credible resources to back it up.

Step 3. Watch out for the things that are obvious.

A common trick that speakers use to gain your confidence in them is to say something that is obvious. You can hear this done in conversation, debates, or read it in persuasive articles online.

What happens is this: a person wants you to agree with their point of view, and they are trying to make their point of view, your point of view. To do this subtly, they are going to say things that you obviously do agree with, then slip in the thing that they are trying to convince you of.

By doing this, you are going to agree with what they are saying because you know what they used to lead up to it is true, and therefore, their final opinion must be true as well.

Let me show you what I mean. You will hear a speaker say something like, "We know that you work hard, that you are trying to get ahead, and you value your money. That is why our product is the best thing for you to invest in."

You know that you *do* work hard, and you *do* try to get ahead, and you *do* value your money. By now, your brain has softened to the speaker, and it is agreeing with what the speaker has to say. So, when the speaker wraps up their speech or article with a pitch for their item, your brain automatically thinks that the product is what you need.

You need to watch out for this. When you see that there are obvious statements being made, put up your guard, and watch for the real reason they are speaking. It isn't going to be hard to find, and you are going to see right through their trick.

Now, you will need to make a conscious effort to make these things a habit of life, but with practice, you are going to see them become a habit for you. You don't want to be a person that is suspicious of everyone that is on the street, which is a temptation for some, but you do want to be smart.

If you follow these 3 steps whenever you are in conversation with someone, or whenever you are browsing the internet, you are going to find that you will make a lot more of your own decisions, and you will feel less like being told what to think and feel.

As we have said before, there is nothing at all wrong with sharing an opinion with another person, or even a group of people, but we don't want you to just go with the flow, or just believe something because that is what everyone else is doing.

You deserve to be a free thinker, and with the help of these steps, it isn't long before you are going to be one.

Chapter 3 – The Benefits of Problem Solving Skills

Critical thinking is the one aspect you are going to use most in your life if you want to take your life from something that is just plain and simple, to the next level. Every person on this planet has problems.

These problems come to us in a variety of ways, and they are different for each one of us, but the point is, every single one of us has problems. Now, many of us sit back, close our eyes, and hope that our problems will go away on their own.

But they don't.

In order to solve your problems, you are going to have to think about them in a critical manner. Pick those problems apart. Look for solutions. Look for ways you can use aspects of the problem to your own advantage.

Think about the problem personally, and independently. Advice from others is great, but at the end of the day, it is still *your* problem, and *you* are the one that is left to deal with it while it is there and ultimately solve it.

The danger of the 'fix it and forget it' method to problem solving

As we mentioned before, society today is both blessed and tarnished with the information that is available on the internet. We all go through our days, and when we need something that we don't know, we consult the internet, fix the problem, and move on.

There is almost a robotic movement that is going on here, and it is one that doesn't aid in the realm of critical thinking. We glance through the solution on the internet, then we close our computer and go on with our day... there is no lesson learned, and nothing that can be applied to another situation.

Of course, a lot of people argue that there is nothing wrong with this. That we will always have the internet with us, and there is no need to worry about actually learning the method because we will always be able to just look it up.

To an extent, they are right about the access to the internet being something that is relatively constant for many of us, but they are wrong in the aspect that we need to develop the skills needed to solve problems.

You are faced with decisions all day long, and without the necessary skills to solve them, how are you going to progress in life?

For example: You can look up on the internet how to make a cake. How to drive a car. Even how to build a car. When it comes to things like that, you are set.

But you can't ask the internet if you should apply for that job that is in the next town. Or if you should invest in your friend's business idea. Or how you are going to apologize to your wife when you feel that you are the one in the right.

These are real life problems, and they are things that Google will never know the answer to, even if you were to ask a thousand times. This is why you need to develop your own problem solving skills, which is largely sourced in critical thinking.

Don't just look at a problem or decision you have to fix. Analyze it.

When you are faced with a decision, whether it be a problem that you need to fix or a decision that will better your life, you need to ask yourself what *you* would do. All too often, when things like these arise, we run to our friends and family to ask them what they would do in that situation.

The problem with this is that what is best for someone else may not be what is best for you. You may opt out of a great job opportunity because your cousin said they wouldn't do it. Or maybe you let your marriage fall apart because your buddy wouldn't try to fix it if he was in your shoes.

Don't get me wrong, advice is always a great thing to have, but you can't base your actions or your life on what other people would do, you have to ask yourself what you would do, and what you should do.

Weigh the pros and cons to any situation. Ask yourself if it would work out better one way or the other. Ask yourself what the risks are, and if you are ok with losing whatever the risk may be if you lose the gamble.

Life is a series of questions and decisions that you need to learn to make, and one that you need to learn to live with the consequences. Critical thinking is a great skill to have, it is going to help you learn how to develop these other areas in your life, and ensure that you are happy with the results.

That is the entire point of analytical thinking when it comes to problem solving and decision making. When you ask everyone else what they would do, you are avoiding taking responsibility for the outcome. If it works out great, you are happy, if it doesn't, then you can blame the other person for not making a decision that worked out great for you.

If you develop your independent thinking skills, then you can make your decisions in full confidence that they are going to turn out great. Of course there is always the risk that something could go wrong, but at the end of the day, you know that you were able to make the decision knowing what you were going in to on the outset.

It is a very different way of dealing with your problems than if you are always asking someone else what they would do. You will learn to stand on your own two feet on any issue, and you will find that you are able to make decisions with confidence.

Chapter 4 – Analyzing Critical Thinking

To better understand the concept of critical thinking, and how you can better develop it in your own life, let's take a moment to analyze critical thinking.

There have been several incredible critical thinkers in history. Here is a list of a few of the greatest:

- Isaac Newton
- Plato
- David Hugh
- Socrates
- Aristotle
- Buddha

Of course these are only to name a few. The list goes on and on with various doctors, philosophers, gurus, and so on. There are two primary things that all of these men, along with the rest of the critical thinkers in history, all have in common.

If you choose to study any one of them individually, you won't have to look very hard before you see that they all:

1. Were deep thinkers

2. Were independent thinkers

There it is again, if you noticed. That word, *independent*. The entire core of the idea of critical thinking is that it is *independent*.

We can't emphasize enough in this book how important it is for you to learn to think for yourself.

We live in a very privileged world. We have all the information in the world... quite literally, in fact, right at our fingertips with the internet. If you wanted to, you can get online, learn how to build an airplane, a light bulb, and why cardinals don't migrate in the fall, then follow it up with the best cake recipe to take to that party tomorrow.

We are given access to more information in less time than ever before. Anyone on the planet with access to a computer literally has anything that they have ever wanted to know right at their fingertips. There are a lot of pros to this, but there is also one major con that stands out above the rest.

We have lost the need to think about things.

You don't have to *think* or *solve* issues anymore. If something is in the way of your progress, all you have to do is pull out your smart phone and Google it. There you have your answer, then you work through the issue, and forget about it.

You didn't *learn* anything, you just got through whatever it was that was holding you back at that moment.

A lot is lost in this way of life. What happens is that we end up adopting the opinion or solution of the person that we read about online, and we don't gain the understanding of how to solve the problem ourselves.

The ability to solve and understand the solution to a problem is key in learning how to use critical thinking to solve your other life problems.

Remember when you were in school, and you were taking geometry? You were given problems and theorems to solve those problems, which you did with ease. You knew that if you followed the formula, you were going to end up with the right answer.

It was all relatively easy to figure out, until you were asked to prove why the theorem worked. This opened up an entire new ballgame, because you weren't going to just figure out the answer, but you were going to figure out *why* the answer was what it was.

When you worked with these proofs, you became a master in the art of geometry. You may not be able to build a building, and you may not be able to repeat every law of geometry as it is written, but you do have an understanding of why things work the way they do in the geometric world.

All of the sudden, circles and squares and triangles all mean something again, and you can make sense of the areas and perimeters. It is more than just knowing *that* 2+2=4... you know *why* 2+2=4.

Sure, this wasn't fun for any of us to do, but at the end of the class, and at the end of the day, we were learning *how* to solve a problem. You *understood* the *why* behind the solution, and that is what set you apart as a critical thinker.

Chapter 5 – Don't Be Afraid to Ask Questions

We have lost a lot of value in thinking these days. It is unfortunate, and it is a new trend in society. If you look back into history, in the Roman Empire and the Greek Empire, and even into the classical times with all of the composers, you are going to see that they were all thinkers.

They didn't write great music, and build empires, and give us all of those great life quotes through Google. They thought about them, analyzed them, and drew up their own conclusions.

You were held in high regards in ancient times if you were a thinker, in fact, that is what many people tried to be. Let's take a moment now to take a look at one of these great thinkers, and see how his method can help us in this modern day not lose the art of critical thinking.

Socrates was a great philosopher and thinker. It doesn't really matter who you are or what kind of education you have, if you are in the world today, odds are you know that Socrates was an ancient man, and that he was a thinker.

Socrates had a method to his genius, and that method was simple: Ask questions.

Socrates was a teacher, and he taught his students to ask questions. He never spoon fed them answers, and he never told them what they ought to think, but he did challenge them in what they did think.

For example, if one of his students were to announce that he believed that music was the way it was for a particular reason, Socrates would ask him why that was so. Or he would ask him if that led to another thing, and the student was free to agree or disagree.

If he agreed, Socrates would ask him why, if he disagreed, Socrates would ask him why.

Socrates wasn't out to point out whether his student were right or wrong, he wanted them to think about why they felt the way they did, and if their conclusions about their subjects were on track or not. Socrates didn't want a world of people that just spat the answers he gave them back out, he wanted a society of thinkers, where each person brought their own skills to the table.

Put it to work! How to apply Socrates' method to your own life.

You can spend your entire day reading what the philosophers did with their students to make them think, but then you have to take a moment and ask yourself how this applies to your life, and what you can do to think better.

If you were sitting in Socrates' class, what would you tell him you were thinking? What questions do you think he would ask you? What would your answers be? You don't have to be in his class to ask yourself these questions, all you need to do is ask them.

Take the time to think about your problems, and any other thing in your life. Don't just blindly accept what you hear or read, *think* about it. Draw your own conclusions, and see where you go from there.

You will be surprised at how many of your problems that seem to be crushing can really be thought through if you sit down and do it.

This can apply to any way that you obtain information. Whether you hear a speaker talking, you watch a documentary, or if you are reading a book. You need to learn to analyze everything.

You don't take a deep book and read it cover to cover without having to pause every now and then to really think about what you have read. If you do this, you are going to lose a lot of what the author intended for you to have.

Instead, read a couple of pages, and set the book down. Wait a moment, and think about what you are reading. Ask yourself questions... think.

1. Is what I am reading true?

2. Do I agree with it?

3. Does it apply to me and my life?

4. How can I make it apply to me and my life?

5. Is there anything the author is trying to convey that I may have missed?

6. How do I feel about this?

Of course you will make the questions more personal to you as you read, and you will find that your problems are going to be more suited to what you are reading, but the method stays the same.

You need to make your life, and your thoughts, intertwined. Make everything you do matter. Think about the information you are absorbing and how it applies to you where you are right now, and how it applies to where you want to be in the future.

When you learn to view life with a questioning attitude, you are going to realize that you can find a lot of the answers in your own mind, and that you can apply these answers to your life.

It will become a cycle for you, but this time a good cycle that is going to lead to good results.

Chapter 6 – How to Avoid Being a Target Audience

As we have already mentioned, there are a lot of businesses out there that prey upon those that don't think for themselves. These businesses all spend their time on elaborate marketing, each with a specific person in mind.

They tell you that if you buy their product, you will be able to run faster, or longer, or your hair or teeth will be prettier, or you will have more friends, or a happier life.

This product "gives you wings" that product "tastes like the rainbow", this product promises that all of your problems will be solved if you have prettier teeth. When you read it in this kind of context, you can probably think of a few more catch phrases that come to mind, and the products behind those promises.

If you have ever been a part of the 'target audience', then it is also likely that you fell into the trap of purchasing whatever the product may be to make your life that much easier.

You bought it, you opened it, and with high hopes you applied it. And waited. You may have noticed some differences, you may not have, but all in all, you find that your life stays mainly the same.

But you did everything that the company said you should, and you even bought their product to achieve whatever it was you wanted to achieve. So what went wrong?

You bought into a gimmick, and became a part of a social group. You bought what you were told to buy, without much thought to the actual results or consequences.

Don't misunderstand, we are not saying that you can't purchase things that you see advertised, or that you can't find things that are going to work for you. What we are saying is that you need to think about the purchase, and think about the advertising.

Be a critical thinker when it comes to your purchases, and make wise decisions. If you don't, you will lose a measure of self-esteem and self-reliance as you only follow what you were told to follow.

How to purchase a product and not be a part of the target audience.

There are some people that take this concept too far... they feel that they can't purchase anything without succumbing to the trap that corporate businesses set forth.

There are actually a few things you can do to ensure that you are thinking critically about your purchases, and that you are able to shop without just mindlessly buying what you are told to buy and shopping where you are told to shop.

Follow this list of questions and apply them to the things that you want to buy. You may want to buy something that is popular, or that there is a lot of advertisement for, and that is perfectly fine.

We are not telling you that you can't ever do anything that is popular, or anything that anyone else is doing, what we are telling you is that you need to think about what you are doing before you do it.

You may want to buy something that is popular and that a lot of other people are buying, or you may not. You can think about it critically, and make a decision based on what you feel you need in your life. If that happens to be the same thing that other people are buying, then that's fine, if it doesn't, that's fine, too.

So here is the list of things that you need to ask yourself when you are buying anything. You can do this when you are at your home before you are even at the store, or you can do it before you make an impulse buy. Either way, it is important that you ask yourself these questions before you buy anything, and you will be thinking critically.

1. What is the marketing of this item?

   Before you buy anything, ask yourself how the item is being marketed. If you see that there are a bunch of happy people, and that the implication is that you need the item in order to be happy, then you may want to consider walking away from it.

   You don't need anything that you don't currently have to be happy, and the marketing companies will play off of the fact that you want to be happy in order to draw you into their schemes. At the end of the day, they don't care if you are happy or not, they just want to get your money.

   Be smart when it comes to the packaging of an item, and ask yourself if you want it, or if you want what they say you will get if you buy the item.

2. What is the company behind this item?

Remember that big name brands are good at what they do, and that they are only after your money. To them, every dollar counts, but they don't care about the individual people that are dealing with the items.

The big name company could care less if you have whiter teeth or if your dog's coat is shiny, but what they do want is more steady customers. Do your research when it comes to the company behind the product.

Ask yourself if there is a better company that you could be buying from, or if you really do have to get it from them. If you are diligent with your research, you are going to find that you have better choices elsewhere, almost every time.

3. Am I happy now, without this item?

If you are purchasing an item to make you happy, you may as well pass it up right now. There is nothing on this planet that is going to make you happy if you have to buy it, only true happiness comes from within.

There are impulse buys that look shiny at the store, and if you stand there for a few minutes, you are apt to think that you will be happy if you but it, but the reality of it is you are just as happy without it as you will be with it, you just have to find that happiness yourself.

4. Do I think that I need this item?

There are two different kinds of needs on this planet. There is the genuine need that you have to have something in order to survive. Clothes, medication, food, shelter... these are all genuine needs.

That new outfit that you think is cute... not so much. There is nothing wrong with purchasing an item merely because you want it, but don't get stuck in the thinking that you need to have the newest and latest and greatest, when the only true needs are very basic.

5. Is this an impulse buy?

   If you didn't have any intention of purchasing an item when you went into the store, then it is an impulse buy. There are times when it is fine to purchase something on impulse, but you have to be careful when it comes to these purchases.

   You only have a certain amount of money in your bank, and a certain amount of space in your home, so do you really need that statue that you didn't even know existed before earlier today?

   Make sure you are certain about the purchase before you make it. Save time, space, and money.

6. Can I live without it?

   This goes along with the same idea of deciding whether or not you really need the item. There are all kinds of things that you will encounter that look bright and shiny on the outset, but you need to think about them before you purchase them.

Again, it isn't wrong to buy something just because you want it, but you would be surprised how many things you mindlessly buy in your week all because of the good marketing that you become subject to in your daily life.

7. Will it make me happy?

There is nothing that you can buy that will make you happy if you are not happy right now, so stop trying, and stop buying into that gimmick.

There are things that you can buy that will be fun, and things that you will have good times with, but there isn't anything you can pay for that is going to bring you lasting happiness.

That is something that you need to have all on your own, and even though the marketing companies all promise that you are going to be happy if you buy this, that, or the other thing, it is all a ploy that they are using in order to get your money.

Don't fall for it.

8. Who am I trying to impress?

Sadly, there are way too many purchases that we make to impress other people. This may be friends, family, our boss, our partner, and the list goes on.

Ask yourself, before you buy anything, if you are buying it because you want it, or if you are buying it because you think it is going to make someone else impressed with you or like you better.

If you have to purchase things to make other people like you, you need to re-think the people that you are hanging around. The real friends in your life aren't going to be impressed with what you buy, they are going to like you for you.

9. Will I regret it?

Buyer's remorse is something that a lot of sellers have to deal with, but you can ensure that you will never have to deal with that in your life if you are careful with what you buy.

If you think about what you are buying before you buy it, then you don't ever have to worry that you are going to regret the purchase. You may need to return it for a different reason, but that is different than you just didn't want it anymore.

Think carefully about what you are buying, and don't be that person that has to think of a reason to return your item.

10. Should I be using the money elsewhere?

There are a lot of people that spend money with other things they need to be buying. They get caught up in the trap that if they buy this or that they are going to be happy, regardless of other things not being paid.

You need to realize that you have your other responsibilities, and no matter what else you buy, you will still have to pay for these as well. You are going to be in a lot more trouble if you buy things on impulse when you still have other things that need to be taken care of, so think these purchases through carefully before you buy them.

Of course you are going to need to make this list your own, and ask yourself questions that are more suited to you, but this is a great list to get you started. Even better, at the end of the day, you have to decide what the answers are, and whether or not those answers mean that you should purchase the item or not.

You might have a rule that says if you answer 'no' to any of the questions that you need to walk away, or you may have another system worked out. Whatever the system is that you are using, you need to make sure that is what you are sticking to when you are purchasing an item.

Chapter 7 – Breaking the Cycle: Becoming Your Own Person

Society in general is a mindless substance. People go through their days, doing what they are told to do, with little though of why they are doing it. They don't ever think of bettering themselves, or trying to do anything new, because all they can think about is what they are told.

If a problem arises, or any form of decision for that matter, they turn to those around them to solve it for them, and even then their friends and mentors don't even think about the problem, they listen to what you are going through, and they tell you the first thing that comes into their mind.

There is no analysis. There are no questions asked. It is merely a mindless answer to a question that was asked from someone who didn't want to think about it for themselves.

To put it bluntly, society is like a herd of cattle that is headed for a cliff. Off in the distance that is a sheer drop, and if you fall over it, you are going to die. These cattle don't know that there is a cliff, but they aren't going to stop to find out. They just keep going and going, and you go right along with them.

Sure, you are going to be fine for a while, as we said, that cliff is off in the distance, but it is drawing closer fast, and you are going to head over the edge right along with the rest of the cattle if you don't change your way.

If you aren't willing to question your direction in life, you are no different than one of those cattle. Your life is headed for destruction, and you can stop it, you just need the wake up call to do it.

Take a few moments right now, and think about your life. We are not trying to be harsh or depressing, but you have to analyze where you are in all of this, and where you can take it if you want to make that change.

We want you to think about everything, and ask yourself, "Why?"

1. What is your religious belief, and why do you believe it?

2. Why do you work where you do?

3. Is your career going anywhere?

4. What is your love life like?

5. Do you love with a passion?

6. Do you make love with a passion?

7. Do you live where you want to?

8. Do you drive what you want to?

9. Think about your exercise routine... do you do what you want to do?

10. Do you eat like you want to?

We know, it is brutal to go through this list, and you may be seeing that there are areas that you need to question. But that is why this is so important... you need to think critically about your life now, and make choices that you have thought about in the future.

Your life is not nearly as fulfilling as it could be, and all you have to do to change it is figure out what you want in life. Ask yourself why you do what you do, and what you can do to change the things that you don't like.

You are not stuck, you can make a change at any time that you want. Maybe you have a lot of things that you need to change about your life, maybe you don't need to change anything on the outside, and you only need to change how you feel about things, and how you are doing things.

Only you can answer these questions, but it is important that you don't ignore them.

Some things that may be right for other people, may not be right for you. It is like we said with the theorems back in school, you can apply rules to your life that you were told are true, or you can

find out for yourself what you know is true for you.

When you take the time to find out what you believe about things, and how you personally feel about it, then life takes on a whole new meaning. You are no longer that lost cow in the herd headed for destruction, you are able to pull back and go your own way.

When you are able to forge your own way in life, you are going to find that you help way more people than just yourself. New ideas are going to spring forth, and so are new ways of doing things. You won't be stuck in the same old way of doing things anymore, and you will find that your life is fulfilling.

Also keep in mind that it doesn't matter where you are in life right now. Young, old, single, married, kids, no kids, CEO of a business or jobless, you can change your path, or at least understand it better where you are, *right now*. So many people get stuck thinking that they are *too* something to be able to make the change that they want to make, but it is never too late until it is over.

Just like with the cow in the herd, you can turn away early on, or you can wait until you are getting closer to that cliff, but the sooner you make the change, the better.

Chapter 8 – Practical Ways to Implement Critical Thinking in Your Own Life

Your mind has got to be going in a hundred directions at once with this. You may be questioning everything, you may even be questioning what we are telling you in this book, and that is good!

You are supposed to question all of this, and see how it fits in your life. Don't run away with this yet, though, there is still a little more that we need to cover. Of course we want you to move on in your own independent thinking, but you may be wondering how to do that.

Let's take a look at some of the practical ways you can implement critical thinking in your own life. Don't worry, we do expect you to question these and make them fit into your own life as they should to be right for you.

1. Stop mindlessly gathering information

There is an entire world out there that is full of information. Whether you are getting if from the internet, from books, from documentaries, from friends and family, or from doctors and gurus.

You need to stop with all of this mindless gathering, and start analyzing truths for yourself. You can get advice from these people, and you can polish your opinion from them, but you shouldn't base all of your opinions on what you hear from other people.

You need to form your own thoughts and opinions, and be comfortable with that.

2. Be a skeptic

Don't be afraid to question. In fact, you *should* question. Question everything. We cannot emphasize enough how important it is for you to question. Ask why about everything.

Don't ever blindly accept anything. Question your religion, your job, your everything. No matter what the subject is, decide how it is right for you, or if it is right for you, and if it isn't, don't sweat it.

3. What's true for one person may not be true for you

This is a great big world, and there are a lot of different people in it. There are those that feel one way, and there are those that feel the complete opposite.

The fact of the matter is: both of them are right. There really is no wrong way to find out what is true for you, you just need to do what makes you happy. Be that person that is ok with being yourself, don't be that person that has to be approved by everyone around them, but instead be that person who is ok in their own skin.

4. Think

Of course this one has to be in here. Of everything that we have been talking about in this book is about critical thinking, so no list would be complete without thinking on the list.

You need to think. No matter what you are doing, don't get stuck in the rut of mindlessness, you need to think. Analyze. Feel. Dream. There is no end to the ways that you can think about things, so think think think.

Of course this is a short list of things that you should do when you are feeling out this new way of life, but no matter how long the list is, there are two main factors that critical thinking can be broken into.

1. Curiosity

2. Open mindedness

Curiosity

No matter how old you are, or what you accomplish in your life, never lose your curiosity. It kind of goes along with the idea of questioning things. You need to always wonder how things work.

Don't just accept that things are the way they are, figure out why. You might wonder how your stove works, or how your car works, or how your particular job affects society in general.

Grow, and keep growing. You only have one life to live, and you are trying to get the most out of it, so learn how things work. If you don't know, look it up. If you do know, analyze.

Open mindedness

Judgement is a hard thing in this world. You are subject to it, and you are a factor in the judgement of others. When you become a critical thinker, you are going to have to break out of close mindedness, and keep an open mind.

We know that there are right things for other people, and there are right things for you, but what is right for them may not be right for you, and that is ok. You don't have to assume right off just because something is different that it is then wrong, or that the other person is wrong for believing it.

You need to learn how to live in this world in a co-existent kind of way. You need to learn to live with others where they are, and still stay where you are at the same time. It takes practice, and it takes work, but you are going to get the hang of it if you are dedicated to do it.

Critical thinking is a spring board to a life that will be fulfilling and rich for you and everyone else that is in your life. It is a process that will take some time to get used to, but you are going to get the hang of it if you are willing to work with it.

You have a new life that is waiting for you, all you have to do is jump in. Just think about it.

Conclusion

Thank you again for getting this book!

I hope this book was able to help you to re-evaluate your decision making skills, and improve your critical thinking in ways that is going to help you in your life.

The next step is to make your choices with confidence. We really hope that you are able to think for yourself, and make choices that reflect that.

This book is meant to show you that you can think for yourself, and make choices that only you agree with. The more you put these things to use, the easier it is going to be to make these choices on your own, and to stick with them.

Independence is a beautiful thing, and the better you get at critical thinking, the more you are going to become your own person. It is an odd thing, thinking that you are not your own person, but until you are able to take a hold of your life and think in your own functioning manner, you are not going to be independent.

If you are serious about making your own decisions, and thinking not only about things, but also thinking through them, you are going to find that the lessons in this book are for you.

We want you to be confident in your decisions, and make choices that you feel are right for you, even if no one else is doing it. You are able to think for yourself, and that is something that is going to serve you well in your life, for life.

Finally, if you enjoyed this book, then I'd like to ask you for a favor, would you be kind enough to leave a review for this book on Amazon? It'd be greatly appreciated! I am a small self published author and need all the help I can get. Thank you very much!

Visit your "ordered products " on your amazon page.

Also. I have a bonus for you on next page. Don't miss that! It could make you a fortune.

If you liked this book check out my other books as well.

Learning:How To Become a Genius & Expert In Any Subject With Accelerated Learning

Positive Thinking: Go From Negative to Positive and Achieve Happiness and Success For Life

How To Be Happy: Alone: The Ultimate Guide On How To Become a Happy and Confident Single, Starting Today

Search for them on amazon.com

Thank you and good luck! And don't forget the bonus on next page!

FREE Bonus!

<u>Want to make money while you sleep?</u>

Visit >>><u>www.GreenSleeper.com</u><<<   to get free tips about how you can make serious money while doing anything else! Sleeping, laying on the beach, traveling, only your imagination is the limit!

At the moment you can get a FREE download of:

"The Make Money While You Sleep Guide"

But hurry up, the book will not be there forever!

Visit My Website And Download It Now! 100% Free! What Do You Have To Lose? Just Search www.GreenSleeper.com In Your Web Browser!

If you don't want the book, read the blog which can teach you a lot of things about business, time management, performance and other things connected to business and success.

49634992R00038

Made in the USA
Lexington, KY
13 February 2016